THE ART OF PUBLIC SPEAKING FOR SUCCESS

CONQUER YOUR PUBLIC SPEAKING FEARS, DEVELOP
YOUR OWN STYLE, AND WOW YOUR AUDIENCE

JIM ALEXANDER

© **Copyright 2021 - All rights reserved.**

The content contained within this book may not be reproduced, duplicated, or transmitted without direct written permission from the author or the publisher.

Under no circumstances will any blame or legal responsibility be held against the publisher, or author, for any damages, reparation, or monetary loss due to the information contained within this book, either directly or indirectly.

<u>Legal Notice:</u>

This book is copyright protected. It is only for personal use. You cannot amend, distribute, sell, use, quote, or paraphrase any part, or the content within this book, without the author or publisher's permission.

<u>Disclaimer Notice:</u>

Please note that the information contained within this document is for educational and entertainment purposes only. All effort has been executed to present accurate, up-to-date, reliable, complete information. No warranties of any kind are declared or implied. Readers acknowledge that the author is not rendering legal, financial, medical, or professional advice. The content within this book has been derived from various sources. Please consult a licensed professional before attempting any techniques outlined in this book.

By reading this document, the reader agrees that under no circumstances is the author responsible for any losses, direct or indirect, that are incurred due to the use of the information in this document, including, but not limited to, errors, omissions, or inaccuracies.

CONTENTS

Introduction   5

1. What is Public Speaking and Why It's Important   11
2. The Basics of Public Speaking   17
3. Your Method for Creating this Change   25
4. How to Deliver the Speech in an Engaging Way   31
5. Making Your Presentations Interactive   37
6. Conquer Your Stage Fright   43
7. Common Mistakes Speakers Make   49
8. How to Get Over Your Fear of Public Speaking Once and For All   55

Final Tips & Conclusion   61

INTRODUCTION

I never thought I would be a public speaker. I always associated public speaking with people who were super confident and outgoing. I was the complete opposite. I was shy and introverted. I didn't think I had anything interesting to say. And worst of all, I was afraid of public speaking.

I was so scared of public speaking that I would get panic attacks before speeches. My heart would race, my palms would sweat, and I would feel like I was going to vomit. It was an awful feeling.

But over time, I learned how to overcome my fears and become a successful public speaker. Now, I love public speaking. I've given speeches at conferences, in classrooms, and even on national television.

According to a study, public speaking is the number one fear in the world. Out of 1,500 people, 74 percent said they fear public speaking more than death. That's a lot of people!

Public speaking is a skill that can help you in your personal and professional life. This book will teach you how to develop the skills of public speaking and conquer any fears about it. It takes time and practice to become a good public speaker, but this is for anyone who wants to be successful at it. Anyone can learn this skill with these tips on vocal tonality and tempo, anxiety-reducing techniques, etc., which are explained in detail throughout the book.

If you want to improve your career or give more convincing presentations at work then read this book because there are many benefits from learning how to speak well in front of an audience...or even just one person!

This book is not for people who are looking to be successful public speakers with no real interest in the topic. This book is also not for people who don't have time to read it and practice what's taught, or for those that want quick fixes. You need to be willing to put in the work to become a good public speaker. If you're interested but unsure about this topic then please read on!

Are you tired of always feeling like you're not good enough?
Do you want more confidence when you speak in public?
Are you ready for a change?

If you answered yes to any of these questions, keep reading!

A skeptic would say that it is impossible to get over the fear of public speaking. They would argue that it is a natural reaction to be afraid of speaking in front of a group of people. They would say that it is something that can't be changed and that you just have to learn to live with it. This may be true for some people. But, for the majority of people, the fear of public speaking can be overcome with practice and a little bit of determination.

This book is still for you even if you don't feel like you are a great speaker. Everyone can be a great public speaker with the right tools and practice. Public speaking is one of the most important skills a person can learn. It can help you in your personal and professional life. You may be thinking, "I'm not a great speaker. I don't know how to start. This book isn't for me." But believe us when we say that everyone can be a great public speaker with the right tools and practice.

1. This book is different because it helps you to develop your own style as a public speaker.
2. This book is different because it provides anxiety-reducing tips to help you overcome any fears you may have about public speaking.
3. This book is different because it provides helpful vocal tonality and tempo tips to help you improve your public speaking skills.

If you are looking to overcome your fear of public speaking, then it is best to read this book from cover to cover. It will provide you with a comprehensive understanding of the art of public speaking and how to apply it in a variety of settings. If you are already familiar with the basics of public speaking, you may want to focus on the sections that deal with conquering your fears and developing your speaking style. Regardless of your skill level, this book is sure to help you improve your public speaking skills.

Public speaking is important because it allows you to share your ideas and thoughts with other people. It can help you build relationships, gain new customers or clients, and even make more money. When you are a good public speaker, people will take notice and respect your opinion more. It can also help you get ahead in your career.

Public speaking is a skill that can be learned. Anyone can become a successful public speaker with time and practice. It is important to have confidence in oneself when learning any new skill. The more you practice, the better you will become. There are many resources available to help improve your public speaking skills. You just need to be willing to learn and practice.

So what are you waiting for? Start learning the art of public speaking for success!

1

WHAT IS PUBLIC SPEAKING AND WHY IT'S IMPORTANT

Public speaking is the process of speaking to a group of people in a structured, deliberate manner intended to inform, influence, or entertain the listeners.

Examples of public speaking could be giving a presentation in a classroom, delivering a speech at a wedding, speaking at a business conference, presenting information to investors, or just talking to an audience on a podcast or vlog. Many other examples could be made, but the point is you will probably be in a position where you have to do some public speaking.

Some people might think that public speaking is not important, but they would be wrong. There are many reasons why public speaking is important. First, public speaking can help you in your personal life. It can help you become a better leader and communicator. Public speaking can also help you build self-confidence and overcome shyness. Second, public speaking can help you in your professional life. It can help you get ahead in your career and make more money. Public speaking can also help you network and land jobs. Third, public speaking is important for your mental health. It can help you relieve stress and anxiety. Public speaking can also make you happier and more productive.

Public speaking is one of the most common fears. Many people are scared of speaking in public. People are scared of speaking in public because it's a very public way to make a mistake. When you're speaking in public, you're in front of a lot of people and you can't hide. If you make a mistake, everyone will know. You're also competing for attention with everyone else in the room. It can be nerve-wracking to stand in front of a group of people and give a presentation.

This fear can hold people back from achieving their goals. They may feel like they are not able to reach their full potential because they are not comfortable speaking in front of others. This can be a major obstacle for people who want to achieve great things. It is important to overcome this fear and learn to speak in public effectively.

Public speaking is one of the most important skills a person can learn, but it's also one of the hardest to master. It takes time and practice to become a good public speaker. But what if you don't have that kind of time? What if you're already struggling with your fear of public speaking? This book will teach you how to be successful at public speaking in just an hour or two per day. You'll learn all about overcoming your fears, developing your own style, and impressing audiences with every presentation.

Developing your own style as a public speaker is important because it will help you stand out from the crowd. When you have a unique style, audiences will remember you. They will also be more likely to listen to what you have to say. You want to be memorable and interesting when you speak in public. You don't want to be just another boring speaker. You want to impress them! If you can impress the audience, they will be more likely to take your advice and recommendations seriously.

They will also be more likely to come back to hear more from you.

In order to be a successful public speaker, you need to be confident. You need to believe in yourself and your message. When you're confident, it will show in your speeches. Audiences will be drawn to you and they will be more likely to listen to what you have to say. Confidence is key when it comes to public speaking.

One of the best ways to become more confident as a public speaker is to practice. You need to practice regularly if you want to improve your skills. The more you speak in public, the more confident you will become. It's also important to get feedback from others. Ask them for feedback after every presentation and learn from their comments. Use their feedback to improve your next speech.

Public speaking can be a very rewarding experience. When you're successful, it feels great. But it's not always easy. There will be times when you feel like you're not doing well and times when you doubt yourself. Don't give up! Keep practicing and learning from your mistakes. You will become a better public speaker over time. And when you do, you'll be able to achieve anything you set your mind to.

Public speaking is a skill that anyone can develop, and it's one of the most important skills you can have in your professional life. The more confident you are as a speaker, the better people will react to what you say. That means practicing public speaking often so that when there's an opportunity for presenting something on stage or during class time, you're not caught off guard and your nerves don't get the best of you.

Here are a few tips on how to be a successful public speaker:

1. Start by understanding your audience. It's important to know who you're speaking to and what they want to hear. By doing this, you can better tailor your presentation to fit their needs.
2. Be confident in what you're saying. This doesn't mean you have to be perfect, but it's important to appear like you know what you're talking about. If you make mistakes, don't worry – just move on and don't let them affect your overall presentation.
3. Be prepared. This is probably the most important tip of all. If you're not prepared, it will show in your presentation. Make sure

you know your material inside and out so that you can answer any questions that come up.
4. Practice, practice, practice! The more you do it, the better you'll become at public speaking.

We'll be going into these topics in subsequent chapters, but it's good to start thinking about them now.

2

THE BASICS OF PUBLIC SPEAKING

Public speaking is one of the most important skills you can possess. It can help you in your personal and professional life, and it's a skill that can be learned relatively easily.

In order to give a great speech, you need to focus on three things: eye contact, body language, and voice tone. If you can make sure that you are engaging your audience with all of these elements, you will be well on your way to delivering a successful presentation.

Eye Contact

Eye contact is so important because it allows you to connect with your audience on a personal level. When you make eye contact with someone, they feel like you are paying attention to them specifically, and that you are interested in what they have to say. This helps build rapport with your listeners, and it makes them more likely to pay attention to what you have to say. In addition, maintaining eye contact will make you appear more confident, which is an important part of public speaking.

In order to have good eye contact with your audience, you need to focus on three things: maintaining eye contact with individuals, keeping a steady gaze, and avoiding distractions. If you can make sure that you are engaging your audience with all of these elements, you will be well on your way to delivering a successful presentation.

Maintaining Eye Contact with Individuals

There are a few things you can do to maintain good eye contact with individuals. First, make sure you are looking at the right person. Try to focus on people's eyes, not just their heads. Second, keep your gaze steady. Don't stare at someone for too long or blink too often. And finally, don't be afraid to break eye contact occasionally to look around the room or scan your notes. This will help keep your audience engaged.

Making Eye Contact with Everyone

It's important to make eye contact with everyone in your audience, not just the people who are asking questions or providing comments. This will help ensure that everyone is paying attention to what you have to say, and it will also help build rapport with your listeners.

Maintaining a Steady Gaze

When you make eye contact with someone, you should maintain a steady gaze. This means that you should hold their gaze for a few seconds before looking away. This will help keep their attention focused on you, and it will help build rapport.

Avoiding Distractions

It's important to avoid distractions when you are making eye contact with your audience. This means that you should avoid looking down at your notes, looking around the room, or checking your watch. If you can focus on maintaining eye contact with your listeners, they will be more likely to pay attention to what you have to say.

Body Language

In order to deliver a great speech, you need to focus on your body language. Your body language can communicate a lot of information to your audience, and it can help you appear more confident and engaged. If you are slouching or fidgeting, your audience will likely get the impression that you are nervous or unprepared. On the other hand, if you are standing up straight and maintaining an open posture, your audience will see you as confident and ready to speak. It's also important to use gestures when you speak; this helps add energy to your presentation and keeps your audience engaged.

In order to use your body language effectively, you need to focus on three things: using open gestures, keeping a positive posture, and avoiding negative body language.

Using Open Gestures

Open gestures help communicate openness and confidence to your audience. When you use open gestures, your hands should be parallel to the ground and your arms should be uncrossed. This will help make you appear welcoming and approachable.

Keeping a Positive Posture

It's important to have a positive posture when you speak. This means that you should stand up straight, with your shoulders back and your head up. This will make you look confident and engaged.

Avoiding Negative Body Language

Negative body language can undermine your message and make you look unprofessional. Some common examples of negative body language include slouching, crossing your arms, playing with your hair or clothes, and fidgeting. If you can avoid these behaviors, you will come across as more confident and competent.

Voice Tone

Your voice is an important tool that can help you engage your audience and deliver a great speech. The way you use your voice can convey a lot of information to your listeners, so it's important to focus on using a clear and engaging tone.

There are a few things you can do to make sure your voice is conveying the right message:

- **Speak at a moderate volume** – if you speak too quietly, people will have trouble hearing you; if you speak too loudly, people will get distracted or even annoyed.
- **Use inflection** – inflection is the rise and fall of your voice when you speak. You can use inflection to add energy to your speech, emphasize important points, or create a sense of urgency.
- **Enunciate** – it's important to enunciate your words clearly so that your audience can understand what you are saying. This means speaking slowly and clearly and pausing between each sentence.

By focusing on these four elements – eye contact, body language, voice tone, and content – you can deliver an engaging and effective speech that will capture your audience's attention.

Now that you understand the basics of public speaking, it's time to put what you've learned into practice.

In order to make a great first impression, be sure to:

- Make eye contact with your audience.
- Use positive body language.
- Project your voice and enunciate clearly. By following these simple tips, you'll be well on your way to delivering a successful speech or presentation.

3

YOUR METHOD FOR CREATING THIS CHANGE

Giving a speech or presentation is one of the most challenging things you can do. It's also one of the most rewarding. Whether you're addressing a small group or a large audience, there are techniques you can use to make your presentation more effective and less stressful. In this chapter, I'll give you five tips to help you get ready for your next speaking engagement.

Practice From an Outline

You should practice your speech from an outline, and not word for word. You want to appear personable, which is what your listeners truly desire from you. They don't want you to read your speech. They don't want you to appear as if you've memorized it;

they want a discussion. So take your notes right away, and then you cut down on them over and over until you're left with a bulleted outline of the key points that you'll write in your final draft. That's all you really need at the end of the day, and that way you have a backup plan to fall back on so you don't lose your spot. You may just check your notes and bounce your rights right back up for a quick presentation from an outline.

That's the most effective approach to follow an outline and then give the impression of an outline. One of the things I'll do so that I don't sound like I've memorized it is every time I practice, I may say it differently on purpose in order to avoid being tempted to memorize, so don't try to devise a word for word. Don't try to memorize only talking points, and then practice from a template like that.

Split Up Your Practice Sessions Over Time

Don't overdo it the night before. Don't overstuff yourself early in the morning before your presentation. I recommend breaking up your practice sessions into three days. The goal is to do practice sessions three times a day. During those three days. I prefer to practice around 10 times before I stand up and speak, and it's much easier to accomplish if you break it down into smaller periods of time.

When you spread out your practice sessions, a lot of wonderful things occur. The first thing I notice is that it soothes me down. It tells me there is still time. So if my first few practice sessions don't go so well. I say, "Hey, there's plenty of time. I'll have a few more days to work out these bugs." Another wonderful consequence is that, say, I practice it three times and then sleep on it. Frequently, I'm washing dishes in the middle of the day while doing other things. My brain comes up with new ways to express something or a quicker approach to get to the point. So, in that downtime, I believe our brains are still working on it and we benefit from it. The additional wonderful thing about dividing your practice sessions is that it assists me in maintaining my composure during the moment. Because I've done this kind of presentation with a previous athlete. It feels like I've been giving this speech for days. So it really helps me keep calm and in the moment. So spread out those exercises three times a day over three days, which is generally sufficient.

Concentrate On Only One or Two Improvements When You Practice

It's logical to work on your structure and outline at first. However, in the next few occurrences, choose just one or two things, like maybe I'm going to work on looking up for my eye contact for example. The next time through, you may concentrate simply on gestures and posture. Make a list of things you want to work on the next time you train. When you try to get it perfect after adding a lot of things all at once, every time you practice, you'll become paralyzed because you can't improve more than one thing or two things in any session. Instead of focusing on the negative, concentrate on ways to improve. After that, start checking off items from your list, and your fundamentals will all be in place before you ever stand up to deliver.

Be Realistic In Your Practice

Keep your practice sessions realistic. Do not, for example, try to isolate yourself entirely while you're practicing, and try to create ideal circumstances. It is not uncommon that people will walk in late or take a bathroom break during your actual presentation, and there will be someone with a lawnmower outside your window.

So, after a few sessions of practicing alone, I bring intentional distractions into it. For example, I'll turn on the television or some music before speaking so that I can distract myself with it. And I'm sure that if I can keep practicing even when things come up and stay focused, that during the actual moment it won't throw me off as much.

Mentally Practice the First and Last 30 seconds of a Presentation

By practicing mentally, I mean visualization, like that of a sports player preparing for their performance. So you're envisioning yourself approaching the podium in the first 30 seconds of your presentation, and then the last 30 seconds how you'll conclude it. Athletes do this with great success. There was a study done by Lori Eckert in the 1980s that revealed similar findings, as well as other studies on basketball free-throw shooting and performance. They discovered that people who merely visualized themselves improving somewhat improved significantly. Free throws improved the most among groups that did both. People who practice free throws basketball saw a modest boost, but athletes who performed both exercises visualized can they improve the most out of any of the groups, according to the studies.

Athletes who did both visualized and practiced free throws had the most growth out of any group in terms of free throws. Visualizing the first 30 seconds and last 30 seconds will significantly enhance your overall performance even if you don't practice it a few extra times.

Giving a speech or presentation can be nerve-wracking, but it doesn't have to be. By following these simple tips, you can prepare yourself for success and deliver an engaging and informative speech or presentation that your audience will love. So what are you waiting for? Start preparing today!

4

HOW TO DELIVER THE SPEECH IN AN ENGAGING WAY

When you stand in front of an audience, whether it's a small group or a large one, your goal is to make sure they are engaged in what you are saying. You want them to listen to your ideas and take away something useful from your speech. How do you accomplish that? There are several things you can do to ensure your audience is fully invested in what you have to say.

Ask Engaging Questions

Instead of simply chatting with your audience, you want to generate a sense of back-and-forth discussion. As a result, you may ask them what they call rhetorical questions that don't require an answer.

During your pause, simply ask the question and they will think about it. Alternatively, you may actually request an answer from them. However, make certain to ask them a simple question that they can easily respond to. It's simple enough, right? All they have to do is maybe raise their hands or shout out a one- or two-word answer. It's not difficult at all. You want to keep things simple. You may also request that your audience participates in some sort of physical activity for you.

Ask Them to Do Something Physical

For example, suppose I tell you to take something from your pockets or that I'd want you to turn through a book that you're reading. I once witnessed a speaker ask everyone to cross their arms. And then, after we all crossed our arms, they spoke about comfort and comfort zone for a few moments. He said, "Okay. Now cross your arms in the other direction." It helped the seeker make his point because there was a little discomfort when you first start trying it when you fold them in the opposite direction. So it really drove home the speaker's argument, by having us perform something physical, immediately made it that much more effective.

Give Your Listeners Something to React to

So it's not just you as a speaker and your listeners, but maybe you put up a relevant quotation or image on a slide. And then you ask them to react to it in some way, like by asking them a question or in some other way that is much more dynamic than just you and your listeners. It's a third part of the puzzle that they're reacting to. First the stimulus, then the response. That will usually get people thinking and get people talking.

Ask For a Volunteer

Ask a member of your audience to come up to the front or stage and demonstrate something with you. When you bring a volunteer up, the other listeners put themselves in his or her place, making them more likely to connect with you and find it far more engaging and entertaining. You can ask them to do something physically at a later time, but bringing the volunteer up is another approach you may use to pique people's interests.

Use a Prop

If I'm talking about smartphones, I want to have a real object to show. A smartphone is way more engaging than a picture of a smartphone. You've undoubtedly flown before if you've ever sat in a seat on a plane. When the flight attendant is showing you how to fasten your seat belts, she or he will use the actual item rather than, say, that little booklet about the seat belts in your pocket in front of you. I don't pay attention to the pamphlet, but I do look at the person holding it. It's a little fascinating how they deal with that seat belt because it's a genuine item rather than an abstract photo.

Use Your Body As a Prop

You may be the prop. Your physical body might serve as a tool for engaging your audience. As a result, the way you move around your speaking area and gesture are all important factors in how you come to life. You might take a few steps into your audience. It's far more interesting to move about than it is to simply stand still the whole time. Now you must exercise caution and avoid walking for no reason. You don't want to walk like you're on edge. You must move with a goal in mind. However, when you move purposefully, it's far more likely to attract others into the conversation and pique their interest.

There are many ways to engage an audience when delivering a speech, whether you want people to act physically or give them something to react to. Whether it's by asking for volunteers, using props, or your own body as a tool in the presentation process, these methods will help get people interested and involved with what you have to say.

5

MAKING YOUR PRESENTATIONS INTERACTIVE

Presentations can be made more interactive by inviting feedback from the audience and asking questions at strategic points. The speaker should pose a question to their audience, get them involved in the topic, and then use that information to continue with their presentation.

In order for this tactic to work well, it's important that you know what type of question will elicit good responses- ones like "What do you think?" or "How does this affect you?" are better than ones like "Do you agree?" which are essentially yes/no questions. It is also helpful if there is a way for people who aren't comfortable speaking up to still participate, like by raising their hand or writing down their response.

This tactic can help keep people engaged and make them feel like they are a part of the presentation, rather than just someone who is sitting and listening. It also allows you to get feedback that can help guide the rest of your talk.

Asking questions is also a good way to check for understanding and make sure that everyone is following along. If you see people starting to look lost or confused, asking a question can help bring them back into the presentation. Just be careful not to ask too many questions, as this can slow down the flow of your talk.

Questions can be a great way to interact with your audience, but make sure you use them wisely!

Invite feedback from the audience at strategic points during your talk to help keep people engaged, and ask questions to check for understanding. Asking the right type of question can get people involved in the presentation and help you get valuable feedback. Use questions sparingly, however, as too many can slow down the flow of your talk.

Another strategy for keeping things interesting is to pause periodically and invite feedback from the crowd, such as "What do you think so far?" or "Do any of these ideas seem promising? Which ones?" You can also ask questions at strategic points during your presentation, such as after you've made a particularly important point. This will help to keep people engaged and ensure that they are following along with what you're saying. Finally, don't forget to leave time for questions at the end of your presentation. This is often where the most interesting discussions take place.

The key is to make sure that the questions you're asking are relevant to the presentation and will actually elicit thoughtful responses from the audience - otherwise, it can just come across as filler. If done right, though, interactive elements like these can really enhance the experience for both you and your listeners.

You can also ask them to raise their hand if you're trying to gauge interest or if you want to know how many people are following along. For example, "How many people here have been pulled over by a cop in the last 3 months?"

There are two great methods for getting audience interaction: the popcorn method, and the ping-pong method.

Popcorn Method

I've used this method countless times now. The most essential thing to realize when attempting to avoid awkward silence is that the best way to prevent it is to create meaningful silence. Before you invite their comments, it's critical to give them at least 5-10 seconds of quiet time so they may think about what you have said.

The popcorn method is when you pose a question to the audience and they answer by popping up like kernels of corn. You can then call on them one at a time to give their response. This is great for getting everyone involved and for gauging how many people are following along. You don't want to talk to one person and have them drone on forever, but you want to illicit little responses from different members of the audience. It needs to be fast-paced, and unpredictable so that the audience knows they'll probably hear a different answer from each person.

But just like a bag of popcorn, you need to take it out of the microwave before it gets burnt. So although you could literally ask each person in the room for their opinion, it's probably better if you just go with 10 people max. Keep between the 3 and 10 range.

You might want to add some of your own commentaries in between some of the responses.

Ping-Pong Method

The ping-pong method is when you get either a ping-pong ball or some other type of ball to throw at an audience member. So now there's audience interaction. So you would ask a question, and then throw this ball to one member of the audience, and when that audience member is done, they throw it to another audience member to give an answer. That way, you're distributing your power as the presenter to the audience. You don't want your audience to feel disempowered but empowered. Sometimes the ball could hit somebody, but hopefully, you've decided to go for a soft ball that won't hurt, so if it happens it should generate some laughter.

But for all of this to work, you have to be really confident in your material. The greatest advice I can offer to any speaker hoping to navigate this volatility is to always be honest. If someone asks you a question or makes a statement that you don't know how to respond to, the best response is "Wow, I don't know how to answer that." You don't know it all, and acknowledging this humanizes you while also moving you to the next level. So the next time somebody shares, what you say next will be listened to more because you're a human and not a sage on the stage.

Both methods are great for engaging the audience and for getting them thinking about the content of your presentation. If you want to make your presentation more interactive, try using one of these methods!

6

CONQUER YOUR STAGE FRIGHT

Do you get nervous before presentations? If so, don't worry! You're not alone. Lots of people feel that way. In fact, according to a recent survey, 95% of all people experience some form of stage fright at least once in their lives and 80% say the fear is still there even when they present frequently. Here are seven steps that can help you cope with stage fright:

1. Form Your Clear Intention

When it comes to stage fright, most people think about anxiety or nerves. Nerves, on the other hand, are generally preceded by confusion or mayhem. When we're rushing around, our thoughts are scattered, and we don't feel centered. It's almost impossible to feel comfortable, and this can cause stage fright before a performance or important meeting.

So, to begin, choose a single clear aim. What is your objective? What are your expectations? What are your goals in terms of what you're about to accomplish? This goal should remove any other thoughts from your mind, and it should be on your mind while you get dressed, drive, or pump yourself up for your time to shine.

For example, if you're going to negotiate, it may be worth getting the customer to sign and remain adamant about the terms. It may be to play my heart out and hit all the right notes if you're going into an audition. It's also crucial to mention that the most essential component of a good intention is to maintain it optimistically. Avoid using words such as "don't" or "no." Instead of "don't make a mistake", say "maintain your confidence."

2. Select a Focal Point

I personally love this technique. Pick a distant, unimportant spot in the rear of the room or auditorium. You'll utilize this point later to extinguish your nervous energy. This is interesting because you're not going to ignore your nervous energy, but redirect it. I'll show you how to do this in step seven, but for now, have a focal area that will be the central point for your nervous energy. You may also utilize a grounding prop if you don't know where you'll be speaking at. I have a pen that I use as my focal point. I picture throwing all of my anxiety towards it, then putting it on the podium or table. It's a really fascinating mental ruse. You become anxious, then picture all of your anxiety into the pen. Then you set it on the table. It deceives your brain into believing you've released your tension. It's strong and easy to understand.

3. Learn to Use Your Breathing to Help You Relax

Oxygen is a kind of wonder drug. It's necessary for life, yet it also eliminates all of the physical symptoms of anxiety. The problem is that we need it to survive. We don't even consider breathing it in. And as a result, when we are nervous without being cognizant of it. Anxiety makes us lightheaded, dizzy, and even more out of breath.

Close your eyes and take a few deep breaths. Second, breathe deeply into your nose and out through your mouth. After that, expand your belly with each breath. This deep abdominal breathing and closing your eyes will assist you in focusing and centering yourself.

4. Reduce Muscle Tension

We tense up every muscle when we become worried. We clench our teeth, stiffen our shoulders, and grasp our arms to the side or in front. Even our stomach shrinks. This is detrimental to blood circulation and anxiety. For this technique, I suggest you gradually relax your body. This is a process that starts at the top or the bottom of your body and works its way down to each muscle one by one. Your feet, shins, thighs, and hips all receive an inhalation one at a time, for example, "relax my head", "relax my shins," and so on. This is a fantastic exercise because it physically relieves tension in your body. It also has the advantage of distracting your mind. Instead of worrying about everything that might go wrong or remembering all the last-minute details, it relaxes the brain.

5. Center Yourself

If we shift our attention to our physical center, it may help us ground ourselves. Consider the location two inches below your navel and two inches below the surface of your belly. This area should be deep within your tummy. We can focus on this spot to calm our minds. You may also consider relaxing this area with each breath, as you did in steps four and five.

6. Repeat Your Process Cue

We discussed your intention at the start of this chapter. This was the aim or target result you wanted to achieve. The process cue is how you want to accomplish your aim. What mental or physical reminder do you want to set for yourself as you evaluate and reflect on your performance? The process cue for an interviewer, for example, might be to smile and ask excellent questions, or the tempo of a violinist may be smooth and good. If you're a public speaker, it could be to keep it upbeat and exciting. Consider how you want to accomplish your objective. What type of tempo do you desire? What emotion do you want to inspire you? This is your process cue. Consider it within as you pep talk yourself when getting ready and during your performance to keep you grounded.

7. Use Your Energy to Your Advantage

Remember the location we chose for the back focal point? This is where you can put anything that's no longer useful to your life. It doesn't work to tell yourself not to be anxious if you're just repeating it over and over. But redirecting that energy might provide a soothing impact. As you get underway with your performance and begin to feel anxious, channel that nervous energy toward the focal point. It'll give you the incredible look of discarding a hefty backpack, and it's an excellent mental exercise to combat anxiety.

Stage fright can be debilitating, but with the right techniques, you can calm yourself down and perform confidently. In this chapter, we've outlined seven different methods that you can use to help center yourself and reduce muscle tension. Remember to focus on your breathing, and keep your energy directed toward your back focal point. If you practice these techniques before your performance, you'll find that you're less anxious and more focused.

7

COMMON MISTAKES SPEAKERS MAKE

If you're a speaker, then there are some common mistakes that you should be aware of. These mistakes could make your speech not as effective and might result in the audience losing interest. They detract from your credibility. They take away from your message and prevent you from effectively conveying your message when you're up in front of two individuals or 200 individuals. This chapter will show you what those mistakes are so that you can avoid them in the future.

1. Not Being Prepared

This is as simple as not preparing for your presentation. I've seen this happen frequently when a speaker will arrive before their presentation and pull out their notepad to begin preparing for it. Some people, on the other hand, are excellent at it. They can go up on stage and deliver a note that is well-received. Imagine if they'd really planned ahead of time and if they'd gone out there and blown people away. Now, there are certain things you simply can't be prepared for. The weather you can't really control, if you get sick, traffic delays, etc. But what you can do to avoid that from even being a problem is arrive early.

I'm not referring to 15 minutes early or a few hours early. If I'm giving a speech at a conference, I usually arrive the day before. Why? Because I need a cushion. It gives me extra time to get ready. There are speakers I know who have actually gone out and partied the entire night before if you can control it, then it is your responsibility.

2. Not Knowing Your Audience

It's as simple as doing some homework. Perhaps it's just a chat with the attendees and finding out who is coming. I've actually given seminars for a women's meeting, and I was aware of what to expect. I knew my audience, and why is it significant? Due to the fact that many of my presentations are geared towards men, I knew I'd have to alter things around. The worst scenario is when a speaker comes in with a prepared speech. And, what's more, it doesn't resonate with the crowd and people are nodding off. The audience's attention is always on their smartphones, not the speaker. Even if he has a wonderful presentation, it won't have an effect if it isn't relevant to the audience or doesn't mean anything.

3. Not Having Concise Points

We're living in an era when people's attention spans have decreased significantly. Make sure to promise them a few points. You don't need to be extravagant in this scenario. I'd say a 30-minute presentation is sufficient. You could reduce it to five, four, or even three points simply by hammering in on those ideas at the start. Don't be embarrassed about repeating yourself. People are frequently distracted, looking at their phones or thinking about something else. It's fine to repeat it at the start or finish, but the objective is to have as few points as possible. When someone breaks away from your presentation, they truly feel like they've learned something.

4. Too Much Dependence on Visuals

You have probably heard the term "Death by PowerPoint" before. Do not be the guy that has the PowerPoint slides with 100 words on them. He's looking over his shoulder to read the PowerPoint slides, and this is his presentation. These are some of the most awful presentations I've ever had to endure, and they happen all too frequently.

"If I put together a fantastic set of 100 slides, I'll be bulletproof," they say. Guys, there's information out there. That is not the purpose of a presentation. The goal of a good presentation is to create a desire among the audience to discover more. I now know that some of you may be giving a one-hour, two-hour, or three-hour presentation. Yes, there may be lengthy presentations, in which case you'll have more time to go into further detail. The idea is that your presentation should be able to survive on its own.

5. Not Getting Honest Criticism

One of the things I do is go back and review my video to see if I make any mistakes or go on for too long. I'm well aware that I rely on crutch phrases. These are things I'm attempting to do in order to improve my speaking. The least you can do if you're going to give a presentation is record yourself and watch and critique yourself, saying things like, "I can do that better." Perhaps take your hand movements down a notch, which is what many presenters like to do. If you can, enlist the assistance of one of your peers to observe you deliver the presentation; after all, they'll be able to time it better than anybody else. If you're searching for a way to get compensated for your presentations, hiring a coach to assist you to figure out what a few changes could have a huge impact on how you communicate might be worth it.

In conclusion, the most common mistakes speakers make are not knowing their audience, having too many points in the presentation, and being overly reliant on visuals. These are all things that can be avoided with a little bit of planning and preparation.

8

HOW TO GET OVER YOUR FEAR OF PUBLIC SPEAKING ONCE AND FOR ALL

There are two types of public speakers, according to celebrated writer and orator Mark Twain. One, those who get scared, and 2, liars. It's understandable that you get apprehensive before and while giving a speech, yet you don't have to let it interfere with your performance. So, now we'll talk about some mindsets and realizations that you should have before presenting, as well as some practical suggestions for managing your anxiety. Let's get down to business and discuss some realizations and practical advice.

The first realization is that you don't appear as terrified as you truly are. I was recently coaching a group of presenters, and one of them ended by stating, "Oh my goodness, I was so nervous," and she had done an excellent job. I didn't realize she was scared. So I asked her on a scale of one to ten how nervous she was. "10 out of 10, I was completely terrified," she continued. I asked the people observing the other contestants how worried she appeared to them. They replied, "two." She did a fantastic job. So just this one realization, on its own, is quite powerful: that you don't appear nearly as worried as you might feel on the inside, and that alone should relax you.

The second understanding is that you're nervous because you've never done anything like this before. It does not imply that you are doing a bad job at the time. Another presenter noted after a recent coaching session, "Oh my gosh, I blacked out. I don't even recall what I did." I'm not sure if she really blacked out, but that's how she said it. She was removed from what was going on. She did a wonderful job despite the fact that she was detached. So just because you feel nervous, it doesn't mean that you're not actually performing excellently. That's something to keep in mind.

The third is that anxiety and enthusiasm are two sides of the same coin. This is the same as if I'm looking forward to performing music for a huge audience. It gets me amped up. So, public speaking is similar to that. You should be enthusiastic. So you don't have to think, "I'm nervous", but instead, "I'm excited." So you have some control over your thoughts in that respect. So, there are a few realizations, and now let's get down to business with some practical suggestions.

The first and most important piece of advice is to practice often. The explanation for this is that during your presentation, 95 percent of the outcomes you see are derived from your practice session. The reason is that if you've prepared meticulously and practiced a lot, the presentation will most likely go well. Even if you're nervous, even if a few minor things go wrong, the outcome will usually be pretty much as planned. Hard work does pay off, and you should make it as realistic as possible. Maybe include a few distractions for good measure. If you make a mistake, don't start again; just keep going. If you're nervous, don't practice speaking to yourself or aloud about how nervous you are because it's possible that you'll do so during the presentation, and that could make things work.

The second key point is to concentrate on your audience and message while you're preparing. If you're overly concerned with yourself, this will irritate you. A comedian is attempting to get people to laugh. They're focused on their punchline, not how they appear. They're committed to getting what they want. They're focused on achieving outstanding results. If you're attempting to teach people, your main goal should be to get them up to speed. Focus on making your point memorable so that it will stick in the minds of others. If you're attempting to convey a message, concentrate on delivering it in such a way that it will sink in and stay with people. Anytime we start thinking about, "How am I coming across?", "I look professional", or "Are people gonna judge me?" It will end up going in the wrong direction. You must completely reverse it and consider your target audience and message.

The third suggestion is to picture yourself performing well, particularly in the first 10 to 20 seconds. When I talk about visualization, I'm not talking about anything weird or experimental or New Agey; what I mean is the way athletes do it. In other words, a batter must put himself in the proper state of mind before coming up to swing in order to picture himself hitting the ball. In the 2001 Super Bowl, St. Louis Rams and New England Patriots were tied 17 to 17 at the end of regulation when Vinatieri kicked his record-breaking 48-yard field goal as time ran out. This is a difficult situation for a kicker. There were no timeouts, and he had only 2 seconds left. He did it, and they won the game. "How did you do it?" they asked after the game. And he replied, "I've made that kick a thousand times before." He said that he practiced it a thousand times in his mind. So then, when you look at it like that, it felt like he was only doing it one more time. When you imagine yourself in the room getting ready, you'll be visualizing the first ten or twenty seconds of the presentation. You're visualizing it working out, seeing how you'll accomplish it, and you'll be ready to succeed.

In order to give a great presentation, you must overcome your fear of public speaking. This can be done by practicing often, concentrating on your audience and message, and picturing yourself performing well. With these tips in mind, you'll be able to present with confidence and achieve outstanding results.

FINAL TIPS & CONCLUSION

Public speaking can be a daunting task, but it's also an incredibly rewarding one. You have the ability to share your ideas and thoughts with the world, and help make a difference in people's lives. In this chapter, we've shared a few final tips on how to be an effective public speaker and make a great impression on your audience. We hope you find these tips helpful as you continue to hone your public speaking skills.

What really helps when it comes to public speaking is learning how to change your perspective. For example, I always tell people that the most essential component of being an effective presenter or speaker is to have a giving attitude. You've heard it, you've seen it, you've done it, and someone thinks others need to hear about what you've done. That is why they invited you to talk. The concern is the number of speakers who show up to take, and it's obvious. People will ask the speaker a question, and the speaker will say, "It's in my book, which you can purchase over there in the back." You could just tell me the solution because you know what it is since you wrote the book, correct?

They do, however, seem to be aiming for book sales. It's a take-what-you-can mentality. Their PowerPoint is jam-packed with their Instagram, email, website, and Facebook presence. So, clearly, they want you to follow them. They want you to visit their website at the end of the presentation, don't they? They have a taking attitude. The first thing they do when approaching you is to provide you with their credentials. It's all about them. It's quite simple and quick to figure out who the benefactor is and who the taker is.

The greatest speakers on the planet, not one of them wants anything from you, even your approval. I'm not sure of any excellent speaker who walks on stage and says, "I'm going to get a standing ovation." You may get one if you earn it and if they decide you have provided them with a lot of value. That is not, however, why you speak. You speak to give value, to give to the audience, without expectation of anything in return.

Another tip to fight performance anxiety is to simply talk, talk and talk some more. Meaning, that public speaking might not be the only way you might face the fear of being embarrassed in public. There's a group known as Toastmasters where you may meet other aspiring speakers and individuals who want to enhance their abilities in a non-threatening atmosphere and give speeches. You can also engage in activities that don't necessarily involve public speaking but still induce performance anxiety. For instance, if you run a podcast or a YouTube channel, then you're public speaking all of the time, just not in front of a physical audience. But still, you'll be getting in great practice. So, anything that makes you feel like you're not performing well, whether it's dancing in public or singing karaoke with your buddies, anything that causes a little bit of fear upfront but then later shows you that the world didn't come to an end even though you did it. That can assist you in gaining confidence, as well as decrease your amount of worry when others believe and those advances feedback into your communication skills.

Another practice-related tip is to record yourself in front of a camera before you give your presentation. For the first few rounds, you don't need to film it since your goal is only to get the information inside your head. So you've memorized the material. After you've gotten the hang of it, then you should record yourself doing every take, then watch yourself do those takes afterward and analyze all aspects of your performance. This is a significant improvement over practicing in an empty room since you're not always aware of what you're doing. The tape doesn't lie, whether it's because you have a nervous tic, you're looking back at the slides too frequently, or you're rushing. So, if you can see your mistakes on tape, you'll be able to figure out what needs to be improved and how much practice you need. You'll be able to practice more effectively and maybe have to practice less than you originally anticipated.

Probably one of the most important pieces of advice I can give you is to know your audience. People in your target audience are likely to fall into one of two categories. The first group consists of individuals who are rooting for you. They want to see you succeed and are interested in your field. These are your supporters. In the second category, you have bored individuals. It's not your fault. It's simply because their thoughts are elsewhere. They're not interested in being there. Even if you do everything perfectly, they'd rather be doing something else and, no matter how excellent your work is, it won't have much of an impact on them. Now, you do want to get as many people as possible into that previous category of those who are interested in your topic. But you should know that the people in the latter group, those who don't care, aren't important. So don't worry about what others will think when you're preparing your speech or when you're up on stage delivering it. That anxiety isn't worth the trouble. If you get constructive criticism for your presentation, later on, that's fantastic, but don't allow it to bother you throughout the speech.

Finally, when giving a speech, concentrate less on the parts of your performance and more on the subject, and also when you're preparing your speech. I discovered that when I'm truly passionate about my topic and the impact I want it to have on the audience, I don't mind so much about the technical aspects of my speech. I don't care about my body language or eye contact because it's as if I'm talking to a dear friend and want them to understand what it is that I know. So the nervousness associated with standing on stage is no longer an issue, and it's focused instead on what I'm saying on stage.

Although public speaking can be a daunting task, following the simple tips in this book will help you become a more effective speaker and make a great impression on your audience. The key is to be well prepared, practice your delivery, and stay calm and confident when speaking. When you do these things, you will be able to engage your audience and deliver a message that is clear, concise, and meaningful. Thank you for reading!